Still We Smile

By Joan M Scott-Lewis

Introduction

Ms. Scott-Lewis loved writing poetry as a child but ceased to do so for many years. She was recently inspired by Mr. Peter Gracey to begin writing again. This book is her rumination on the highs, lows, surprises, and complexities of a well lived life. The author is very interested in getting your perspective on her work and hopes you will make this book a conversation piece. As you read each poem, think about what it is saying to you. Then follow these three steps:

- ❖ choose a poem that resonates with you.
- ❖ identify your reason for choosing that particular poem.
- ❖ send a message to sljoanm@gmail.com

Prayer

Dear Lord,

It is my earnest prayer that each reader will be blessed upon reading these poems. May they be inspired, encouraged, and motivated to make changes that enhance their lives and the lives of others. Lead them to seek a personal relationship with you. Please bless their homes, their families, and their lives. I ask this in the name of Jesus.

Amen.

Dedication

I lovingly dedicate this book to my parents Lilybell A. Scott and Wallace A. Lewis who are both deceased.

I also dedicate it to my dear children Richard, Denise, Michael, and Stephen, to all my offspring, my family, my friends, and my past students.

A special thank you to my family and friends for encouraging me in this journey and for being such supportive critics.

About the Author

The author is a woman of strong faith. She is proud of her beautiful family, and her heritage. She is a cancer survivor and an overcomer who credits her faith as her source of strength.

Ms. Scott-Lewis enjoyed a happy childhood on the island of Jamaica where she was born. She attended Rollington Town Primary School in Kingston, Jamaica. Her family migrated to London, England when she was quite young. She went to school in England, was married, and gave birth to her four children there. She later moved to Brooklyn, New York.

Ms. Scott-Lewis currently resides in Florida. She holds a Bachelor's degree in Business Administration and a Master's degree in Teaching. Ms. Scott-Lewis is now retired, but worked as a New York Stock Exchange licensed stock broker, and a Florida (OCPS) licensed educator for a number of years.

She is a member of Rejoice in the Lord Ministries, Apopka and a member of the Jamaican American Association of Central Florida.

Table of Contents

Shades of Green 1

PINK 2

Build a nest in me 3

YOU 4

We Shine 5

Free 6

Love 7

GONE 8

Hope 9

Sanctified 10

Don't try to limit Me 11

Please don't break my mommy 12

Walking with the Angels 13

Resistance 14

Fire and Ice 15

Promises to keep 16

Having Fun 17

Still We Smile 18

Those Words 20

The Tempter Within 22

Plant Good Seeds 23

Perfect Rhythm 24

The Truth 26

Higher Ground..27

The Plan 28

Envy Unleashed 29

Forgiveness 31

Wisdom...32

Great Expectations 33

The Orchestra..34

HE IS! 35

Reach for the Stars.................................36

The Kingdom 38

Determined 40

The Heart 42

Desire..43

I am Man, I am Woman...........................44

Shameless 46

He's The One..47

Shades of Green, By Joan M Scott-Lewis

Shades of green piercing the soul,

unveiling minefields of fear and doubt.

Penetrating daggers of regret.

Longing for what belongs not,

torments from day to night.

Consumed with thoughts of fierce design;

not seeing the forest for the trees.

Aimlessly, focusing on stolen seeds,

the sunken spirit bleeds.

Filled with promises of birth denied,

as stifled shoots lay bare.

Relent, insidious mind relent;

to greener pastures veer.

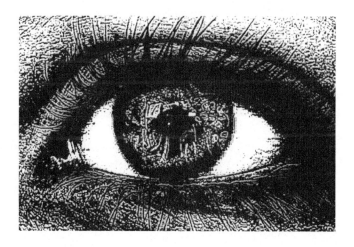

PINK, By Joan M Scott-Lewis

Perfect!

But so out of sync.

Filling the void with flowery thoughts.

Nothing is done, for no one can think.

Believing that all is intact;

hearts and senses disguised.

Judged by appearances only.

Pretty in pink.

Caught in a melee of lies.

Build a nest in me, By Joan M Scott-Lewis

When the rivers of life seem dry and dim,

and the leaves are brown and bare.

Build a nest in me!

When thunder roars and lions pounce.

Build a nest in me!

When friends forsake and showers fall.

When nothing is, as it should be.

For now, and all eternity.

Build a nest in me!

YOU, By Joan M Scott-Lewis

The sun setting in the sky;

clouds of brilliant hue.

Reaching to attain,

just another glimpse of YOU.

Thank YOU for Your Spirit,

that glows deep within.

I am my best me,

because of YOU.

No stain or blemish can ever dim,

my hope and desire to glorify YOU.

The sky, the seas, the mountains,

the winds already do.

More than air or breath,

I pant after YOU.

For there is nothing

that lasts -

except the aura of YOU

We Shine, By Joan M Scott-Lewis

Like a diamond, glows in the mine:

We shine.

Like a penny glossy and new:

We shine.

I shine, so you can shine too.

Your talents, your poise

I celebrate you.

Enhancing your glow.

Igniting each spark;

your brilliance to show.

So often we shine,

you in your small corner, and I in mine.

A mere speck in time and space.

But when we combine;

we light up the world:

And darkness will decline.

Be present, be bold.

Flames flickering bright.

Unswerving WE WIN,

when we ALL choose to Shine.

Free, By Joan M Scott-Lewis

Dancing in the rain;

playing in the snow.

Swimming in the ocean;

going with the flow.

Breaking free from manacles:

Where did they go?

Only those unyoked

by mental slavery;

will ever truly know.

Free at last, we cry

free at last.

Speak it, feel it,

know it, deep within.

Rise up from your slumber, my friend.

Let the dream begin.

Love, By Joan M Scott-Lewis

Aroused by your beauty;

mesmerized by your winsome smile.

Unearthing dormant feelings;

numbed for a while.

I am my beloved,

my beloved is mine.

Eyes of oceans deep;

heart and mind entwined.

I drink you in, I drink you in,

like sweet, sweet wine.

GONE, By Joan M Scott-Lewis

You left me on a Sunday;
shaken and confused.
Filled with guilt and sadness:
Purpose yet unused.
Signs noticed, yet ignored.
Careless naivety.
Shattered dreams:
Painful memories of regret.
Where are you now my love?
Left to wonder, What if? If only?
Filled with doubt to ponder.
From time to time,
thinking of what might have been.
Asking why - you left me in your prime.

You left me on a Sunday; decades later.
The month, the day, the same.
Yet, sadness and guilt remain.
Did so much for you:
But, wishing it was more.
Gypsy girl, you deserved a world
of peace and grace;
to match the beauty of your face.
Assured of where you are, my love:
Languished in your mansion
prepared just for you.
Three score, ten, and more:
Still searching for a sign.
Voice echoing in my soul -
you left me in God's time.

Hope, By Joan M Scott-Lewis

Rivers of tears; mountains of fears.

Wearing us down; crushing our crown.

We tried and we tried.

We cried and we cried.

Disillusioned and torn;

battered and scorned.

Look to the hills,

where hope springs eternal:

The empty heart to fill.

Whispering, "Help I thee give,

come hither and live."

Sanctified, By Joan M Scott-Lewis

Did not know; yet

sanctified.

Brought to the water,

but bones would not move.

In immobility, blessed and set free.

Grace is more than sufficient for thee.

Touched with such presence.

Filled with purpose anew.

Showered in power and made in like image:

There is so much to do.

Divine authority granted

to accomplish each task:

Consecrated, Sanctioned, and True.

Don't try to limit Me, By Joan M Scott-Lewis

Soaring like an eagle - Emboldened.
Free to fly solo,
but I'll gladly take you on this spree.
Just don't try to limit me.
Don't clip my wings;
Don't trim my sails.
With eyes ahead, all
systems go.
The power within propels me,
to worlds unknown:
Visions yet to behold.
I fly so high;
motivated to be me.
Beyond the clouds, I persevere.
It's tenacity
that keeps me here.
The air is filled with electricity.
The wind and rain - my best friends.
This storm - it enables me to higher ground.
Gliding over mountains,
and hurdles set before me.
These challenges - merely an opportunity.
Daunting insecurities -
have nothing to do with me.
Blind negativity
will not disrupt my Flight!

Please don't break my mommy, By Joan M Scott-Lewis

Please don't break my mommy.
Don't pull her hair.
My heart is aching;
you don't seem to care.
Wanting to protect her - just don't dare.
Trying to break the mold:
But, what can I do?
I'm only six years old!

Please don't break my mommy.
Her eyes are filled with fear.
Your thundering screams at her,
I just can't bear:
Her knight in shining armor,
I wish I could be.
I want to be bold:
But, what can I do?
I'm only six years old!

Please don't break my mommy.
Her tears are real.
Wishing you could see,
that when you break mommy -
you're destroying me.
I want it to stop;
I want to set her free.
So much anger I hold:
But, what can I do?
I'm only six years old!

Walking with the Angels, By Joan M Scott-Lewis

Walking with the angels,

wings extended.

Tears all gone-

Gathered with the holy throng.

Streets of gold;

beautiful and free.

Sentiments of wonder,

surrounding me.

Meeting my heroes,

and my heroines too.

Wrapped safely in the arms,

and comfort of You.

Basking in serenity;

floating gently on soft clouds.

Vision of pure bliss.

Resistance, By Joan M Scott-Lewis

Resistance comes with the dream.
Resistance comes with success.
Resistance comes with favor.
Continue to do your best.

Character is developed,
from the worst of days.
In hard times and failures,
resistance prevails.
The pit - Just a part of your story,
to finance your journey.

Nothing good comes easy.
Your dissenters,
will be your collaborators!
Your haters, your elevators!
Adversity spurs you forward.
Be prepared to excel.

Resistance is real.
It fuels the dream.
Developing muscles of pure steel.
Focus on the plan and purpose.
Though wounded by deceit;
be still and know,
you will conquer the feat.

Fire and Ice, By Joan M Scott-Lewis

Gripping tight, hard cold vice.

Suffocating cinders of hot timber.

None can the heart retire;

to feelings warm and tender.

For neither lasts, emotions to temper.

Burnt out flames fading;

melted fluids draining.

Dust we are and dust will remain.

Recognize the forces within:

Burning passionate and combustible.

Frigidly fragmented, internal deep freeze.

Minds of ash and hearts of steel;

having a permeating effect.

Tissues scared by compounded

opposites of destruction.

Like vaporized steam:

Here today, tomorrow gone.

Disintegrating,

into a reckless picture of extremities.

Promises to keep, By Joan M Scott-Lewis

Promises to keep.

Deliverance from pain.

Lives to waken from deep sleep.

Eyes to dry, not in vain.

Weeping endures but for a night.

Joy peeps through tomorrow;

eliminating sorrow.

Coming in a voice made loud;

hearken to the cry:

You will live and not die,

and never beg bread:

Take hold of the promise;

proclaim it far and wide.

Having Fun, By Joan M Scott-Lewis

Chasing rainbows in the sky.

Looking for the good times.

Leaving secret scars.

Bright lights blinding.

A word to the wise:

But who is listening?

Candles burnt at both ends.

Nothing left to lose.

Sleepless nights of discontent;

filled with broken dreams.

Little time to make amends.

Well, we were just having fun,

when all is said and done.

Still We Smile, By Joan M Scott-Lewis

Smiling makes the shackles fall.
Secure and safe from valleys deep,
and the darkest of shadows.
Though arrows aimed to cause distress
with words of vile contempt;
would seek to harm, and see us crumble:
Our smile will not relent.

Through it all we smile.
Grateful to be present,
for even a while.
Our smile may seem naive to some,
and lay oblivious to others.
Yet choose to smile we will;
no matter the circumstance.
There lies within a strength of power;
keeping us humble.
Sustaining quiet confidence.

Amidst the tempest we persist.
We will not buckle.
With heads held high,
we will not sink, nor will we flinch.
The battle is already won.
The victory is nigh.
Above the waters of despair
we float; like lilies on a lake.
Nothing can pull us under,
nor keep us down.
(next stanza)

What we show may
not be our experience.
We have suffered much;
endured even more.

Still, we smile.
Still, we dance and sway.
Moving to melodies so divine:
Smiling each step of the way.

Those Words, By Joan M Scott-Lewis

Those Words!

Words like thunder;

deafening the senses.

Rampaging insults of anger and rage.

Those Words!

Words like lightning;

flashing, frightening, fiery bolts.

Shocking the system,

and piercing the mind.

Those Words!

Words like tornadoes;

twisting, turning, terrifying.

Violently tearing

at the fabric of the soul.

Those Words!

Words like hurricane;

flooding waters, winds of force.

Vicious arsenal of destruction.

(next stanza)

Those Words!

Let us weather those words;

poised to trample young dreams,

of promise and light. So fraught with pain.

Those Words!

Exchange those words,

for words of kindness and peace.

Purposed to inspire, and poised

to usher warmth and delight.

The Tempter Within, By Joan M Scott-Lewis

Resist the tempter within.

A vicious tyrant.

An insidious rebel, without cause;

that only the still small voice can contain.

Make the choice -

check temptation at the door.

Make it your footstool,

not your tower.

It will control you, if you let it.

The inner tempter -

comes in subtle ways;

Beguiling and discreet.

Expect to be tempted:

But you are not alone.

There is a plan and prescription;

a means of escape.

Examine your motives:

Dig deep and discern.

Plant Good Seeds, By Joan M Scott-Lewis

Plant good seeds!

Let them grow;

sprouts of promise to bestow.

Make it rain;

watch the blossoms swell.

Do your best to honor God,

and teach your children well.

Plant good seeds!

Model virtue,

and determination.

In time, a harvest will come.

Civility will spread like wildfire;

good fruit to manifest.

Sow grace, not strife,

and you and yours

will be surely blessed.

Perfect Rhythm, By Joan M Scott-Lewis

Align yourself to the rhythm.

Get in perfect harmony;

to gain insight and understanding.

Fullness of life is yours,

when you prioritize your position.

You will receive

that which is for you:

But you must stay close,

to get the anointing.

Proximity is everything.

Attune your life and grow.

Untether yourself from

your misaligned pattern.

Aspire to live in fulfillment.

Rewrite your dance card.

Shift to the true flow,

and go with the tempo.

Move to the sweeter beat,

to synchronize your feet.

Timing is everything.

(next stanza)

Let there be praise inside you;
for all that God has done.
He has the perfect plan,
to turn your mourning to joy.
Step into divine authority, and
walk in victory and favor:
Intentionally equipped.
Live in maturity
and obedience.
Surrender is everything.

The Truth, By Joan M Scott-Lewis

The Truth is foundational.

I am! He said,

the Way, the Truth, the Life.

None can come, but by Me.

Share the good news -

So, the world will know;

that The Truth

will never change or deviate,

and comes alive in the hearts

of those who believe.

Beautiful, pure and cleansing,

compassionate and kind:

The Truth,

the very Author of Authenticity!

Higher Ground, By Joan M Scott-Lewis

The source of a limited life,

and a hopeless existence

lies in the valley of despair.

Move from that which tears apart:

That sphere,

of depression and fear.

Be confidently assured:

A relief fund for the soul

can be found;

that loosens the ties,

that have you bound.

Move on to higher ground;

where safety and healing abide.

The Plan, By Joan M Scott-Lewis

Things not working

according to plan; wants

unfulfilled.

Hopes frustrated and repressed.

Playing author of our souls;

making deals for goals.

Disappointment flares,

as objectives go unaddressed.

Anger and resentful sets in.

No longer listening, mind spinning.

Not realizing there is

no genie in a bottle.

What can be gained?

For there is no understanding,

nor recognizing who the

True Author is.

Take hold of the plan,

made by The Creator, not by man.

Seek and you will find,

the roadmap that leads to the Way.

Envy Unleashed, By Joan M Scott-Lewis

Envy unleashed!

A vulture on the prowl;

ruthlessly scoping its prey.

Preparing to pounce,

with strength and speed.

Leaving nowhere to run:

No hope of escape.

Envy unleashed!

An unknown stalker;

mercilessly tormenting its victim.

Clothed in fury,

unpredicted and unprovoked.

Unacquainted,

yet strangely familiar.

Envy unleashed!

A broken sewer;

excreting filth and waste.

A vile conduit,

of stress and fear.

Spewing toxic onslaughts

of destruction.

(next stanza)

Envy unleashed!
A rabid assassin;
foaming at the mouth.
Bound and determined;
charged with spite and rage.
Resolved to accomplish
its cruel mission.

Forgiveness, By Joan M Scott-Lewis

Forgiveness, an incredible journey.

A complicated history

of acts of grace.

Acts that accumulate in time.

Filled with steps to secure your peace.

Humanize the perpetrator,

and shower them with kindness.

Forgiveness is priceless.

Endless as the universe.

Gentle as a cool spring breeze.

Soft as silk, and pure as gold.

It will serve

to release, refresh,

and revive your soul

Wisdom, By Joan M Scott-Lewis

Give us wisdom, lest we stumble.

Remove the veil

from our defective lenses;

that keeps us blinded by ignorance.

Anoint us with wisdom

and grant us courage;

to be a blessing, here on earth.

Show us the breath

and length of Your will.

Transform our lives.

Illuminate our vision:

Our destiny to fulfill

Great Expectations, By Joan M Scott-Lewis

Not what we imagined,

nor hoped for.

Not meeting

our great expectations.

A King riding on a donkey:

Not in a carriage.

Reconciling broken relations;

salvation to bring.

The government

on His shoulders.

Our worldly expectations dim,

in His presence:

As disappointment turns to favor;

when we know

who He IS.

The Orchestra, By Joan M Scott-Lewis

Symphonies of motion.

A masterful painting

comes to life.

A fine-tuned ensemble;

gliding like smooth blades of grass.

Depth of dimension,

with power and passion.

Ebbing soft and low;

building to a mighty crescendo.

A breathless tapestry of harmony:

But one wrong note

can ruin the sound.

Pulling in a different direction.

Shattered and scattered,

unconforming.

Marching to your own beat;

informed by a foreign drum.

HE IS!, By Joan M Scott-Lewis

Turned water into wine.

Changed death to destiny.

Made whole by a touch

of His garment.

Created a way for you and me.

Placed the weight in our favor.

Such credible,

and incredible evidence of love.

HE IS!

Our hope for years to come!

Lord of Lords!

Prince of Peace!

Rock in a weary land!

All in All!

Be not dismayed,

whatever the tide

HE IS that HE IS!

Reach for the Stars, By Joan M Scott-Lewis

Reach for the stars;

where love and passion combine.

Let your heart and mind collide.

Not looking back,

unless to lift another on the climb.

Know that you are divinely purposed,

and never undermine

the power within:

The thrust that helps you ascend.

You are designed to stay on track.

Strive to live vibrant and free.

Abundant in life, forever to rise.

Grace testifies to your pattern

and progress.

Reach for the stars,

with anticipation.

Give praise to the one who

prepared and destined your course.

Write the vision and make it plain,

and hope will come alive.

(continue stanza)

Be confident and assured

that you are blessed.

Take hold of opportunities

that may never come again.

From day to day,

take one step at a time

on the ladder of success.

Illuminating with light;

radiating efficacy.

For you have earned this moment.

Now humbly assume

your rightful position in the galaxy.

The Kingdom, By Joan M Scott-Lewis

Holding to promises:

Faithful and true.

Fearlessly declaring the truth.

So much for the Kingdom,

yet to do.

Please transform me:

Change my heart.

For that is my world's

best chance.

To be a light in the darkness.

Salt of the earth.

Grateful for vision.

Thankful for new birth:

Instructed to learn:

Commissioned to teach.

Building a kingdom,

that nought can impeach.

Spiritual fruit will tell me apart.

(next stanza)

Reaching humanity;

the message to convey.

My will to submit,

from day to day.

Gallantly advancing;

the mission to fulfill.

Delighted to go.

Equipped and armored;

to pursue the fight.

Determined, By Joan M Scott-Lewis

Determined I am,

to do as I pledged.

To stay on track.

To focus on the road ahead.

To raise the bar.

To level up:

And never by fear be led.

It is my turn.

It is my time.

Like a sprinter in a relay,

run the race I will.

Determined I am,

I will not fold;

nor will I falter:

But will keep pressing on.

Resigned to meet the challenge.

I will not turn tail;

nor my plight bewail.

For this race I will surely win

if I continue as promised;

to do my best to reach the goal.

(next stanza)

Determined I am,

to hold fast.

I am not the first leg;

nor am I the last:

But my intention is clear

I will carry on:

Till I reach the one

that takes hold of the baton

and continues the run.

Till then I will do all that I can

to uphold my task, until my time is done.

The Heart, By Joan M Scott-Lewis

The heart, a complicated organ

of contradiction.

A reservoir of deception.

A symbol of true love.

Deceitful, and desperately wicked:

At times misunderstood.

A vital source of strength and life.

Yet can so easily be broken.

The seat of decision making,

where visions take flight.

So, guard your heart,

with all your strength and might.

Be careful not to react

to every emotion.

For the heart is a chest,

for what we treasure.

For all we hold dear.

Yet it is also a home

for grief and sadness -

A habitat for fear.

Desire, By Joan M Scott-Lewis

Climbing through the window

of the mind.

No resolve or peace to find.

Caught in the fragment

of each pane.

Senseless emotions to reconcile.

There is no escaping

the torture of past pain.

Wishing and hoping for better days.

Nothing ventured,

nothing gained.

Catching at sunlight

through the haze

While fleshly frames,

contain the picture of a promised landscape

Yet, ungained.

I am Man, I am Woman, By Joan M Scott-Lewis

I am Man, I am Woman.

I am all I was formed to be.

A nation uniquely proud

and resilient.

Made from the finest of stock.

Survivor, and reviver.

A remnant established to rise.

To rise above the snares

and violence.

If you can imagine:

Being captured, raped,

and plundered.

Placed in chains;

the existence of my ancestors.

Who struggled far too hard,

and died way too young;

for me to express and promote

my humanity.

The devil held tightly onto the reins,

and kept them engulfed in shame.

Telling them they were inferior,

and the lowest on the food chain.

Yet still they found the grit to rise,

above the ashes of despair,

and unimaginable cruelty.

(next stanza)

I am Man, I am Woman.
I will rise.
With eyes fixed on the prize,
focused on the unseen.
I will run, I will run well
to the mountains and beyond.
For indeed I must reach
the mountaintop,
to honor their dreams.
Though some would seek to muffle me,
and stifle my resolve;
I will not be silent
nor will I live in the shadows:
But will walk in absolute freedom;
without fear of earthly hindrance.
To be all, I can be.
For I am Man, I am Woman.
So, I will strive for as long
as blood runs warm in my veins
to do what is necessary:
And never succumb
to anyone or anything,
that tries -
Again, to enslave me.

Shameless, By Joan M Scott-Lewis

Slashing, stinging, spiteful tongues;
shameless and slanderous.
Casting poisoned daggers in the dark;
leaving collateral damage..
Does your vilifying others
fill you with hidden pride,
or cover your own private impotences?
Inadequacies you try so hard to hide;
while pointing fingers, and finding fault:
Standing in absolute judgment;
consummate judge and jury.
Looking down your self righteous nose
with vitriol condemnation.

Shamelessly focusing on the speck
in the accused person's eyes;
conveniently ignoring the plank in
your own.
You may think you have it under control:
But be careful how you tread.
Remember when you dig a pit
for your accused,
you must dig two instead.
For the law of God and nature stands true:
You will reap what you sow, and
the havoc you cause to others today,
will inevitably - return to you.

He's The One, By Joan M Scott-Lewis

Tired and worn; burdened by life's stresses. Feelings of

rejection and abandonment,

weighing heavily on your mind.

Living dangerously close to the precipitous edge.

He's the One!

Objectified and abused; nowhere to turn.

Thinking this world would be better

without you; that there is no hope for tomorrow.

For no one understands.

He's the One!

Consumed by self destructive; blinded by trauma and fear.

Searching for a safe place; an anchor for the soul:

There is a better way:

Love God, love self, love others.

He's the One!

Overwhelmed by the day to day.

Concerns of the world bogging you down:

Your children, your finances, your failures;

problems that press and hold you hostage.

He's the One!

(next stanza)

Abused and neglected;

trying desperately to hold on.

Perceiving yourself as hopeless and less than.

He promises beauty for ashes.

So press the restart button:

He's the One!

Printed in Great Britain
by Amazon

24844424R00033